Ever
Insig

C000110302

*Disappointment
and Loss*

Claire Musters

CWR

© CWR 2020

Published 2020 by CWR, Waverley Abbey House, Waverley Lane, Farnham, Surrey GU9 8EP, UK.

CWR is a Registered Charity – Number 294387 and a Limited Company registered in England – Registration Number 1990308.

The right of Claire Musters to be identified as the author of this work has been asserted by her in accordance with the Copyright, Designs and Patents Act 1988.

For a list of National Distributors, visit cwr.org.uk/distributors

Unless otherwise indicated, Scripture references are taken from taken from the Holy Bible, New International Version® Anglicised, NIV® Copyright © 1979, 1984, 2011 by Biblica, Inc.® Used by permission. All rights reserved worldwide.

Other versions used: NLT: New Living Translation, Copyright © ©1996, 2004, 2007, 2013, 2015 by Tyndale House Foundation. Used by permission of Tyndale House Publishers Inc., Carol Stream, Illinois 60188. All rights reserved.

Concept development, editing, design and production by CWR.

Every effort has been made to ensure that this book contains the correct permissions and references, but if anything has been inadvertently overlooked the Publisher will be pleased to make the necessary arrangements at the first opportunity. Please contact the Publisher directly.

Printed in the UK by Linney

ISBN: 978-1-78951-276-2

Dedication

To my mum, Sue Keir, who taught me so much about resilience of faith in the face of constant physical suffering, despair, disappointment and loss. Now with the Lord, I am sure she is enjoying pain-free time with the One she clung to so resolutely and faithfully.

Note from the author:

I wrote this devotional at a time of personal loss, but the Covid-19 outbreak occurred while the book was still in production. This situation has touched every nation and every individual in some way, causing many of us to come face to face with disappointment and loss in various forms. Although we may have experienced collective and individual pain, I still firmly believe that the messages of lament and hope I have shared from Scripture remain true for us all, as we find hope and resilience in God and His Word, just as Christians have done throughout the centuries.

Introduction

Many of us face times of disappointment as well as loss. Whether it is the loss of a loved one, a job, a relationship, a dream, the disappointment of being let down by a friend, of being overlooked, of health issues, of not marrying, not being able to have children or of life simply not working out as we had imagined it would, we can all struggle intensely when such things happen. We may be encouraged to be honest, but we may also be expected to be able to move on quickly. The result is that many of us are not equipped for dealing with loss and disappointment well. As Revelation 21:4 says, one day: 'There will be no more death or mourning.' However, until then, we are living with the tension of the 'now and not yet' of the kingdom of God. Sometimes we see breakthrough, but at other times have to live with searing pain.

I was halfway through writing this devotional when I got a call to say that my mum was in her final moments. The rest of my writing was done sat by her bedside as she spent days, rather than hours, moving from this life to life with Jesus. That was just like her: she taught me more about faith and perseverance in the midst of pain than anyone else I know, and her fighting spirit kept her alive much longer than experts expected.

Whatever specific disappointment or loss we each face, it is vital that we allow ourselves the space to process it well. The first stage of processing difficult emotions is acknowledgement. I have had to acknowledge that, at times, my disappointment has been due to unrealistic expectations I placed on people, situations and even God. While facing that, the resulting hurt was still very real and I had to work it through with God.

The Bible is full of examples of God drawing near to His people when they were suffering deep disappointments and heartbreaking losses. I pray that we can learn from their experiences, and take heart in the overriding message of love and hope.

I do not pretend to have all the answers, but I offer up my thoughts and prayers in the hopes they will be of some help to you on your own journey. We cannot escape difficulties in this life, but we can be confident that we 'will see the goodness of the LORD in the land of the living'. So, as you begin this devotional, I encourage you to, 'be strong and take heart and wait for the LORD' (Psa. 27:13–14).

He knows

READ: JOHN 11:1–12,32–35

'Jesus wept.' (v35)

This is the shortest verse in the Bible, and also feels like the most appropriate place to start. We will be looking at passages from the Old Testament and then the New Testament over the next 30 days, so we will return to the story of Lazarus and his sisters later, but for now, let's just sit for a while, simply acknowledging that Jesus felt emotion – deeply.

When we are facing deeply intense, negative emotions, we can feel as if no one understands. Often, God can seem distant from us too. We can wonder why He has allowed what we are going through, and why He feels so far away. And yet, however enveloped we are in the searing pain, however great the chasm we feel there is between us, the truth is: God is *always* there. In Hebrews 13:5, He promised: 'Never will I leave you; never will I forsake you.'

What we see in the story of Lazarus, though, goes even further. Jesus not only appeared in the saddest, messiest part of human experience; He felt the emotional pain of loss too. While we may find it perplexing that He stayed where He was for longer when He heard Lazarus was sick (because He knew God wanted to show His glory by resurrecting him; see verse 6), it is vital that we don't miss the details in the story: He was deeply moved by Mary's weeping (v33) – and wept Himself.

There is much in this story that I wrestle with (which I will share later), but I do gain comfort from the fact that Jesus' example here shows me that it is OK to not only feel, but also express, pain. Disappointment and loss can affect every part of us; as we will look at more closely tomorrow, it is important not to bottle our emotions up.

I also believe that verses 33–35 reveal that Jesus doesn't stand far off, but is willing to come and weep alongside us. I do not know the difficult path that you may be walking right now, but I do know that Jesus does, and He empathises with what you are going through.

Dear Lord Jesus, while my heart may be heavy, I choose to take comfort from the fact that You were not afraid to show emotion. Help me to allow myself space to express how I am feeling. Amen.

The Lord gives and takes away

READ: JOB 1:1–21

'Naked I came from my mother's womb, and naked I shall depart. The Lord gave and the Lord has taken away; may the name of the Lord be praised.' (v21)

There is a Matt Redman song, *Blessed be Your Name,* which talks about the Lord giving and taking away. I have known how difficult it is to sing those words when going through a severe sense of disappointment or hopelessness, and know others who have suffered desperate losses and have struggled to sing it for a time. But still there is an eternal truth that lies within the lyrics, which Job acknowledges here.

When wrestling with the idea of loss, Job is often a biblical figure cited – not because his story contains answers, but because he suffered such a catalogue of losses. I think one of the most important things his story does is reveal the lie that, if we suffer loss, whatever is happening to us must be our fault. This man was totally 'blameless and upright' (v1) and had known God's blessing in his family and work. When the devil suggests to God that Job may not be so upright were he to suffer, the devil is allowed to take from Job's family and livelihood – but not to touch Job himself. Job responded by expressing his grief in a culturally appropriate way, tearing his robe and shaving his head. He didn't skip the emotional pain of loss, but he did continue to acknowledge the sovereignty of God.

I don't know whether I would praise God so quickly if I suffered to the extent and intensity that Job did, but I do know that, even if I were to lose everything else around me, my faith is the bedrock on which I have built my life. The pain would be excruciating, suffocating and overwhelming, but the truth is this: everything we have in this world is a temporary gift from God that we simply steward. Job is absolutely right to say: 'Naked I came from my mother's womb, and naked I shall depart.'

Lord, it may seem like a harsh truth, but it is true that I came into this world with nothing and will leave the same way. Help me to accept that, and not to cling to anything so tightly that I would curse You if You were to take it away. Amen.

Be careful who you listen to

READ: JOB 22:4–11

'Is it for your piety that he rebukes you and brings charges against you? Is not your wickedness great? Are not your sins endless?' (vv4–5)

Job's friends began well; they chose to support him in his grief by coming alongside him and grieving too. We are told in Job 2:13 that, because his grief was so great, they didn't say anything but simply sat next to him.

Sometimes, our sense of loss is so overwhelming that we need people who are willing to show up and sit with us, without trying to explain everything away. The latter is, sadly, what Job's friends went on to do. The bulk of the book of Job is a lengthy discussion between Job and his three friends, in which they try and find reasons for why he must have suffered so greatly – and he refutes them all, becoming more and more despondent as he does so.

It may be that you have suffered a huge loss or disappointment, and, however well-meaning, friends or church workers have said things that have caused further hurt as you know they are simply not true. In our humanity, we find it hard to accept that sometimes things seem to happen for no explicable reason, and, sadly, we can grasp at wrong explanations. If you know that the words people around you are speaking to you are untrue or, at the very least, unhelpful, you can choose not to take them on board. The Bible teaches us to 'take captive every thought to make it obedient to Christ' (2 Cor. 10:5) and so you can discard that which you know is not meant for you. I recently experienced this when I initially felt guilty for questioning something a friend said out of misplaced kindness, but then God gently invited me simply to sit with Him.

God often speaks tenderly to us in the midst of loss; sometimes He challenges our assumptions (as we will see tomorrow), but He doesn't heap condemnation upon us. When we are processing difficulties, it is helpful to ask for His discernment so that we don't listen to the wrong voices.

Lord, I know that, in my fragile humanity, I might say the wrong thing to someone suffering. Help me to forgive those who have done that to me, and to let go of the wrong statements spoken. Give me Your wisdom to work through this well. Amen.

Questioning God

READ: JOB 42:1–6

'You asked, "Who is this that obscures my plans without knowledge?" Surely I spoke of things I did not understand, things too wonderful for me to know.' (v3)

Throughout his discourse with his friends, Job addressed God, questioning why He had allowed such suffering into his life. Reading through the whole book, you can see his desperation was building. His friends' explanations didn't hold up to scrutiny, as Job knew he had lived an upright life, and so he demanded to be given a chance to defend himself.

I think we can be frightened of expressing to God our inner questions, but Job was very direct (Job 7:20)! Interestingly, God did not answer his questions in the way he might have been expecting. Instead, He turned the questions around onto Job to get right to the heart of the matter. God highlighted Job's ignorance of the natural order of the earth and revealed His sovereignty (Job 38:4). When Job finally got a chance to speak back to God, he simply had to acknowledge that there were mysteries he couldn't understand; knowledge that was beyond his capability.

It is really humbling, yet also freeing, to get to the point of acknowledging that we won't understand everything that happens in this life. It doesn't make the acute sense of disappointment and bewilderment any easier, but it can cause us to consider what our response to any form of suffering is. We saw on Day 2 that the devil asked to inflict loss on Job because he thought that Job only praised God because he was blessed. Job's three friends thought he was suffering because God was judging him. The younger man, Elihu, who also talked to Job (see Job 32–37), had a better explanation – that suffering is a way that God teaches and refines us. While this is true, it cannot explain away all pain and loss. God's view is that He longs for us to trust Him for who He is, not what He does. Can we say that we do?

God, I admit that I can be confused as to why You allow some of the pain in my life. It can be so hard to deal with. But I want to ask You to help me trust You simply because You are my God and King, and for no other reason. Amen.

In the face of betrayal

READ: 1 SAMUEL 24:1–22

'I have not wronged you, but you are
hunting me down to take my life.' (v11)

I have gleaned so much from David's life, so
am going to take a few days to ponder different
parts of his story. First, a quick reminder about
David: he was anointed by Samuel (see 1 Sam. 16)
to be the next king of Israel, and soon after
fought and conquered Goliath (1 Sam. 17). Even
though God had recognised the good in his
heart when choosing him (1 Sam. 16:7), he faced
disappointment throughout his journey to the
throne – and beyond. When Samuel asked to
see all his sons, David's father, Jesse, didn't
even bother to get him back from the field until
prompted. And when he went to the battle lines
where Goliath was mocking the Israelites, his
brother accused him of being conceited. Having
defeated Goliath, Saul kept David close to him,
but was continuously jealous, knowing David
was now God's anointed.

It must have been excruciating for David
to have to wait for his kingship, especially as
Saul, in his later years, kept trying to kill him.

In chapter 24, it looks like David has his chance for revenge; to finish things, once and for all. His men interpret this opportunity as being from God – but David thinks differently. When he gives in a little, he is immediately conscience-stricken, and openly tells Saul what happened.

What a challenge; when we are disappointed by others' actions, what is our response? Do we look for ways to point out their shortcomings, or do we extend a hand of grace? At times, we too, will face what appears to be treachery: at other times, we may encounter thoughtless wounds from a friend. How we respond is important. It can be so hard to contemplate the idea of forgiveness when we have been disappointed deeply by others, and yet that is often the key to us being able to walk free. God gently invites us to let go of the burden of hurt and give it to Him.

Lord, I know there are times when I am so disappointed in others that I want to retaliate in some way. Help me to learn from David to keep my heart pure, and to keep short accounts with others. Amen.

Owning up

READ: 2 SAMUEL 12:1–23

'David said to Nathan, "I have sinned against the LORD."' (v13)

I want to tread very carefully, as I know people who have been told that their difficulties must have been caused by their sin or lack of faith – when they were not. We can judge one another too quickly, as we saw Job's friends do. However, it is an inescapable truth that some of the pain we experience in life is due to our own mistakes.

While David was known as 'a man after [God's] own heart' (see Acts 13:22), he was still tempted in the area of lust – and gave in. Having taken Bathsheba for himself, and then ensured her husband's demise, he may well have thought he had got away with it all. However, God spoke to the prophet Nathan, and he challenged him. We may feel that God's judgment was harsh – to spare David's life but take his son's – but what I want to focus on is how David is a flawed but relatable character.

David has always been close to my heart. As a worship leader and church leader, I have long appreciated the qualities he expresses and the songs he penned. But I also relate to his massive failures and attempts to cover them up. I, too, gave in to the temptation of an extramarital relationship and faced the consequences. At one point, nearing the age of 30 and living back with my parents, I had to face the very real possibility that I had thrown away everything I loved – my husband, my home, my church and my work.* I had to repent before God and allow Him to be Lord over every part of my life again, and then spend some very difficult months working through the pain and disappointment that had led to my actions, as well as seeking forgiveness from others – and extending it where necessary. I would never wish to walk that path again, and to know how much I hurt others is still hard. However, it was in that time that I experienced God's love and grace in a way I never had before – direct from Him, but also from those around me.

Lord, as David prayed in Psalm 139:24: 'See if there is any offensive way in me, and lead me in the way everlasting.' Amen.

*I share more about this story in *Taking Off the Mask* (Milton Keynes: Authentic, 2017).

God our shield

READ: PSALM 3

'you, LORD, are a shield around me, my glory, the One who lifts my head high.' (v3)

When Nathan rebuked David, God declared: 'Out of your own household I am going to bring calamity on you' (2 Sam. 12:11). Even though David would have understood that connection, the pain he must have felt when making the decision to flee Jerusalem, when his son Absalom rose up against him, would have been excruciating (see 2 Sam. 15:13–14). Bad enough to have been hunted down by Saul – but this time it was his own son who had turned the people against him and seized power! Which is why it is quite remarkable that Psalm 3 was penned by David during this same period. In this psalm, he does not shy away from describing what was happening, but he also declares who God is.

As I've mentioned, we will look at the way the Psalms give us instruction on how to give voice to both our pain and faith later, but, for now, note how remarkable it is that David could 'lie down and sleep' (v5). He knew that it was God who was sustaining him and, while facing severe loss (the loyalty of both his family and many subjects) and huge disappointment, he could still testify to the trust he had in God. While he knew 'tens of thousands assail me on every side' (v6), he did not fear.

One of the amazing lessons I think we can learn from characters in the Bible is how disappointment does not have to turn us away from God; in fact, it can actually draw us towards Him. Rather than questioning and accusing, we can remind ourselves of who God is, and the fact that, although mighty and holy, He is not distant, but wants to commune with us. He can provide rest and comfort in even the most painful of times.

Whatever you are facing today, take a moment to meditate on the fact that God shields and sustains you. Even in the midst of intense difficulties, it is true that we have nothing to fear.

Lord, I thank You that however fierce the battle is around me, however battle-weary I feel, You are my shield. I declare to myself today that I need not fear because I am Yours. Amen.

A persistent hope

READ: 1 SAMUEL 1:1–11

'In her deep anguish Hannah prayed to the LORD, weeping bitterly.' (v10)

Hannah was childless and faced constant personal shame and the contempt of others. Being unable to conceive in biblical times carried social stigma as it heaped embarrassment on the family. Not only that, she was taunted daily by her husband's other wife, Peninnah.

I have not suffered the terrible pain of infertility, but I have close friends who have, and I know the deep-seated anguish that it can carry. Proverbs 13:12 says: 'Hope deferred makes the heart sick'; that is a very accurate description of the longing that is so keenly felt. I am so sorry if that is the disappointment you are facing today.

What can be hard to understand is that the writer here chooses the words: 'the LORD had closed her womb' (v5). We are clearly being told that God had a purpose in this pain, although often, when we read a passage like this, all we can empathise with is the torment. Even though she had a husband who loved her dearly, her heart was aching. There seems to be no clear answers as to why God allowed her pain to carry on for so long... just as, often, there aren't easy answers for us today.

Hannah lived at a time when Israel had been taken over by the Philistines, and many of the people had forsaken their faith in God. Hannah's husband, Elkanah, was one of the few that still made the trip to sacrifice at the tabernacle every year. Travelling with him, Hannah took time to pour out her soul to God. She learned how to cling to Him through her sorrow and plead her cause. She is in our Bibles today as an example of godly persistence; going before Him in prayer, again and again, despite the heartache in her soul. I am sure it was painfully difficult at times, but we can learn to do the same. We have a God who longs to draw us close; who wants to be right with us in the midst of the mess and heartache.

God, I don't fully understand Hannah's story and why she had to suffer the pain of ridicule on top of infertility. But I am inspired by the way that she brought her pain to You again and again. Please help me to be as persistent. Amen.

Resolute – in anguish and in joy

READ: 1 SAMUEL 1:12–28

'Do not take your servant for a wicked woman; I have been praying here out of my great anguish and grief.' (v16)

Most of us would have understood if Hannah had become bitter over the treatment she had received. Not only was she ridiculed by those around her, God hadn't answered her prayers and even the priest assumed the worst of her. But she resolutely held her ground and it seems reached a new place of peace through doing so. Look at verses 15–18 again. She had been pouring out her grief, but, after speaking to Eli, suddenly got up and ate, no longer full of sadness. We aren't told what happened; whether what Eli the priest said to her encouraged her and/or, in her honest outpouring, she reached the place of leaving the pain with God. Perhaps she learned the lesson of true humility – giving up her right to understand why she was having to wait.

I attended a conference with a speaker that challenged us on this very point. She asked whether we cling to what we think is our 'right', demanding God give us answers. This can cause our hearts to grow cold and bitter. The alternative is to set our minds to hope in God despite difficult circumstances, and lay down our rights to know the reasons behind any delay and disappointment. That day, I decided to take a very honest look at my motivations, desires, hopes and dreams – and the self-pitying attitude that can appear. I hope that I can learn to be as persistent, honest and humble as Hannah.

When Hannah was finally given a baby boy, Samuel, she was just as resolute in her joy, handing over her longed-for child to Eli, just as she had promised God (which must have been so hard). She had no idea that God's purposes had been outworked in the waiting – her son had been born at exactly the right time to grow up and be the one to lead the Israelites back to God and to victory against the Philistines (see 1 Sam. 7).

God, there is so much to learn from the life of Hannah. Please help me to lay down my rights to understand everything that happens to me, and to reach that place of calm trust in You. Amen.

Two people, two responses

READ: RUTH 1

'The LORD has afflicted me; the Almighty has brought misfortune upon me.' (v21)

Naomi and her husband originally left their home country due to a famine. Having experienced the loss of her husband, but also the joy of seeing her sons grow up and marry, Naomi then lost both her sons. She went from being married and secure to being a widow and childless. The pain must have been agonising – and relentlessly ongoing.

I chose this passage next, as I want us to continue reflecting on our responses to difficulties, and to honestly take note of what can happen when bitterness takes root. Naomi was overwhelmed by her own grief – she had no space to consider anyone else's. She tried to send both her daughters-in-law away, but gave in when Ruth determined to go with her (see vv16–18). Naomi was honest about where she was at, but allowed her bitterness to swallow her up so completely that she actually named herself 'bitter' (that is what Mara means – see vv20–21). She had begun to blame God for everything that had happened.

Contrast Naomi's response to her pain with Ruth's – I think often we overlook that she too must have been grieving the huge loss of her husband, but she showed remarkable faith to put her trust in Naomi and Naomi's God. She chose to leave everything she knew to follow Naomi to a new land – even though Naomi wasn't particularly supportive of that decision.

None of us are immune to feeling deep anguish, and it is important to be honest about our emotions (to God, but also to close family and friends). Do we have 'Ruths' in our lives, who are willing to stick by us even when we are overwhelmed?

The contrast between these two women's responses invites us to carefully consider whether we have stepped over from grief into bitterness. Ruth didn't even know God personally at this point in their history, but she was able to demonstrate to us that faith is still possible in the midst of loss and sorrow.

Lord, help me to keep a check on my heart, so that I do not become bitter or blame You for the sadness I experience in this life. Help me to recognise the 'Ruths' You have brought into my life. Amen.

Lasting legacy through the pain

READ: RUTH 3:1–6

'she went down to the threshing-floor and did everything her mother-in-law told her to do' (v6)

While Naomi returned to Judah totally engulfed in her own grief and resulting bitterness, Ruth seemed more able to see beyond her own pain. Having lived with Naomi while married to her son, she knew the qualities that Naomi possessed deep down. We see those begin to reappear when Ruth first encounters Boaz. Naomi may have blamed God for what happened to her family, but her faith hadn't disappeared. Her immediate response to Boaz's initial kindness to Ruth was to thank God (see 2:20). And at the start of chapter 3, we can see that her self-focus was beginning to shift, as she started to think about Ruth's future (v1). If you read through the whole of Ruth, you will see that Boaz became the kinsman redeemer (a foretaste of Jesus' role in our lives), marrying Ruth and securing her future. But it was Naomi's knowledge of tradition, and the wisdom with which she counselled Ruth, that kick-started the process. Her very actions would change her relationship with Ruth (and she had no guarantees that her life would improve too), but she sought the best for Ruth. She had been open with her pain, and was just as open with her faith and with her counsel, leading the way for Ruth to truly understand how to walk with God.

It is incredible to reflect on the genealogy at the end of the book of Ruth (4:18–22). Boaz was Obed's father; Obed, Jesse's father; and Jesse, the father of David. This is the bloodline into which the ultimate kinsman redeemer, Jesus, was to be born! Out of such pain and heartache, which had necessitated both women bravely giving up all they had known and then clinging on to faith in the midst of their grief, a world-changing genealogy was continued. While we may not see the repercussions of all that God is doing through our difficulties in our own lifetime (see Heb. 11:13), we *can* trust Him. We *can* continue to interact with Him each and every day, whatever the pain that has come to our door.

Lord, I acknowledge that You are orchestrating the whole of history. I am amazed that, ultimately, out of Naomi and Ruth's loss and pain, You came to earth. Help me to trust You with *all* the details of my life. Amen.

He sees you

READ: GENESIS 16:1–16

'She gave this name to the LORD who spoke to her: "You are the God who sees me"' (v13)

This story can seem quite odd to our modern eyes. While Abram and Sarai had followed God's call to leave their home country of Ur, they couldn't understand how He would fulfil His promise to make their descendants as numerous as the stars (see Gen. 15:2–6). In Genesis 16, we see they took matters into their own hands, using Sarai's slave as a surrogate. This was the custom of the day; we are not told how Hagar felt about it, although it could have meant a change in her position – for the better – as she would have been seen as a concubine or second wife. Hagar did take advantage of the situation to lord it over her mistress (Gen. 16:4). It all became a mess, just as our own relationships can at times. The women seemed to be full of jealousy, hurt, pain and disappointment. Sarai was heartbroken at being childless, and Hagar was mistreated by a couple whom she had trusted (previously she would have seen evidence of their faith and how their whole lives were centred around following

God's call). Hagar may have viewed it as far easier to take her chances in the desert than stay in that toxic environment.

Incredibly, God went to Hagar in the desert – and He will do that for us too. He called her by name, and then asked her a question that gave her dignity (v8) – as well as the chance to reflect on what was happening. God cared about her as well as Abram and Sarai. She got a glimpse into His character, and called Him 'the God who sees me'.

He didn't promise an end to Hagar's disappointment. In fact, He asked a great deal of her – to go back to her mistress (v9). It was hard, but, fuelled with the knowledge that He saw her, Hagar did what He asked. This always speaks to me of the treasure we have as believers. No matter what disappointment we face, however hard the thing God asks us to do is, we have the security of knowing we are seen... and loved.

Lord, even if You don't change the circumstances around me, I choose to remember that You see and know all I am going through – and You love me deeply. Amen.

Not alone with our future

READ: GENESIS 21

'Lift the boy up and take him by the hand,
for I will make him into a great nation.' (v18)

Once God blessed Sarah and Abraham
(previously called Sarai and Abram) with Isaac,
there was some enmity between the sons
(Hagar's son, Ishmael, mocked their celebrations
– see v9). This time, Hagar and her son ended
up in the desert because they were sent away.
When they had run out of provisions, she sat
a little way away from him, so that she didn't
have to watch him die. She must have been
overwhelmed with a sense of disappointment
and loss – as well as confusion. She had done
what God had asked of her, but look where
they had ended up anyway. She may have felt
let down by Him too: when He had asked her
to return to Sarai, He had given her a promise
for her future (and beyond): 'I will increase
your descendants so much that they will be too
numerous to count' (Gen. 16:9). But now it looked
like they would simply die in the desert.

Have you ever been in that position?
Wrestled with disappointment so much, but

stuck with what you believed was God's will in a situation – only to experience more heartache? We can really be caught off-guard when that happens, but I believe Hagar's story shows us how God is with us, even when life doesn't work out as we expect. It doesn't mean that life will be easy, but here we see His tender care even in the hard place – God was moved by Ishmael's tears and comforted Hagar, and also practically helped them by providing refreshment. He also reiterated the promise that He would make Ishmael into a great nation; a promise I'm sure Hagar struggled to hold on to at times while they remained in the desert. Ishmael grew up and married while they were still in that desert place (and, interestingly, must have reconciled to a certain degree with Isaac as Genesis 25:9 tells us they buried their father together). Even if the place we are in seems dry and disappointing – and that season lasts far longer than we had hoped – we have the promise of a future with God.

Lord, I don't understand why You might sometimes ask me to stay in situations that are really hard, but I thank You that my future lies secure in You. Amen.

Getting personal

READ: PSALM 13

'How long must I wrestle with my thoughts and day after day have sorrow in my heart?' (v2)

I love the fact that God gave us the book of Psalms because, even if those around us expect us to be calm and collected at all times, He knows we *will* feel deep emotion – and this book shows us that it is OK to express it!

It may be that simply by reading through the Psalms, you are inspired to write your own – or that they give you the confidence to speak out how you are feeling to God with total honesty. The psalms of lament make up over a third of them all and, while they are all slightly different, they offer us really valuable guidance for our own personal laments.

Many commentators talk about the lament psalms taking us on a journey: not only leading the speaker/reader into the darkness but also through it and out the other side. While they do differ slightly in their approaches, many follow a similar format to the one shown clearly in Psalm 13, and you may find it helpful to follow that approach if you feel unsure how to take your pain to God.

The Psalms address God directly. While there may be really searching questions included, the way they are written shows that there is an intimacy to the relationship – however hard it is, the psalmists know how important it is to keep communicating. We see this happening in verse 1: 'How long, LORD? Will you forget me forever?' The writer continues with what can be seen as complaint (vv1b–2) before adding in a request (vv3–4). This seems even more personal, with the use of 'my God'. I believe this shows us we can be really personal and specific.

There is often then a shift in focus – a transition has occurred. The psalmist moves on to a statement of trust (v5), and often this includes praise (v6). When we are in despair, we can feel it is too difficult to worship, but we forget that being honest before God is a form of worship, as we are inviting Him into every part of our lives, and remembering His character does not change when our circumstances do.

Thank You, Lord, that You have provided help for us to connect with You in times of intense emotion. Help me to allow You into the bad times as well as the good. Amen.

Collecting our tears

READ: PSALM 56:1–8

'You keep track of all my sorrows. You have collected all my tears in your bottle. You have recorded each one in your book.' (v8, NLT)

God does not stay far off when we are suffering but nor is our suffering wasted. He not only looks on us with compassion and care, but beautifully tends to our outpourings of pain. In this psalm, we see David lamenting his circumstances. As we saw yesterday, the Psalms give us an incredible template for coming to God with our pain and here, we can see David tells God what is going on, and declares that he will continue to trust in God even though he may be fearful.

I just love the image that follows his effusion of words. When I am feeling overwhelmed, I often come back to this, mainly in the New Living Translation because it is so incredibly vivid. There has been much over the past couple of years that has caused me to weep uncontrollably – it just happens and there is nothing I can do about it. I sometimes feel that

God turns the tap on, knowing that I need to express my sadness and sense of loss so much. But the beautiful thing is, I've come to realise that no tear is wasted. No sorrow goes unnoticed. God gently and carefully collects each tear, and records each sorrow.

I don't understand why He does this, but I do know that He can work through suffering and pain to make us more like His Son, and Jesus was known as the suffering servant. As Paul indicates in 2 Corinthians 4, this human life is fleeting and our bodies fragile, but God works through it all. Much of my pain was in watching my mum slowly wither away, desperate to be with Jesus as every breath got more and more difficult. She clung to this verse: 'Though outwardly we are wasting away, yet inwardly we are being renewed day by day' (2 Cor. 4:16). Yes, we may suffer sorrow and pain; yes, we may cry, what seems like, endless tears. But this is part of our story, and God lovingly records it all.

Lord, I acknowledge that tears may be a regular part of my journey, as I learn to process my disappointment and loss. Thank You for reminding me that no part of what I go through goes unnoticed. Amen.

Honesty before God

READ: PSALM 77

'Has his unfailing love vanished forever?
Has his promise failed for all time?' (v8)

It may be that you feel you really don't know how
to speak to God in your pain. Can I gently suggest
that you spend some time flicking through the
Psalms until you find one that echoes how you
are feeling? Engaging with a psalm can help us
to face negative emotions that we've previously
pushed below the surface, so that we can process
them. It helped me so much, when I was in
despair over my sin, to find these verses: 'My
wounds fester and are loathsome because of my
sinful folly... I groan in anguish of heart' (Psa.
38:5,8). I was so thankful that someone had been
able to express what I was feeling – and that I
wasn't alone. I was so disappointed with where
my life had ended up; so disappointed in myself.
I spent time simply reading, wrote the verses in
my journal and also used them in my sorrowful
conversations with God.

Psalm 77 is one that I have found particularly
helpful since. The psalmist says that he cried
out to God, but he 'would not be comforted' (v2);

there is a description of deep anguish. There are then six rhetorical questions; while the writer may not really believe these if he stopped to reflect on them, he is acknowledging it is how he is feeling. I sense some anger in there, which is an emotion I was surprised to feel in a time of grief.

The psalmist then chooses to remember what God has done in the past – and reflects on who He is. As he does so, his perspective changes.

This psalm reveals it is OK to voice the questions our deep pain might bring up. It is when we get stuck there that we can get caught up in bitterness, unforgiveness etc. But lament is the bridge between our pain and belief in God – and here we see it is by remembering the miracles, and works of faithfulness from God, as well His characteristics, that the psalmist is helped. God's power and love anchor the second part of the psalm; they are anchoring the writer's very soul at the same time.

Lord, I thank You for the gift of lament and how it helps us to find our way to You even in the midst of deep despair. Teach me to use lament to anchor my soul when I am struggling. Amen.

Speaking to our souls

READ: PSALM 42

'Why, my soul, are you downcast? Why so disturbed within me?' (v5)

I do believe that when the Church doesn't engage with the practice of lament we all miss out on a vital part of our faith. Personally, I have found it so helpful while processing my own sadness and pain in recent years.

The writer of Psalm 42 begins by expressing how deeply he needs a touch from God. The image of a deer panting for water is such an evocative one and I am immediately reminded of times when I, too, have felt that dry and desperate. It appears that the psalmist has felt that God is far away from him, especially when his foes rub it in and say, 'Where is your God?' (v10). Sometimes, when we think back to how things used to be, in the good times, it just causes us more upset.

What I find so interesting is how the writer then turns and speaks directly to his soul. This may not be something that we are used to doing but it makes a lot of sense. We live in a world where we are constantly being bombarded by messages: through social media, TV, magazines, in the workplace etc. And what goes through our minds can be a mix of all that we have taken in from those sources, as well as our own inner voice – and the accusatory voice of the devil. While the Holy Spirit does prompt us, we have seen we are also told to 'take captive every thought' (2 Cor. 10:5). Speaking to our souls can be part of that process. We can keep a check on what we are thinking, and also speak into our thinking too. As the psalmist does, we can remind ourselves to trust God; in fact, lamenting openly in this way is a real act of faith. As Mags Duggan says: 'The practice of lament has been described as the most profound demonstration of trust in a loving God because it demonstrates an unwillingness to let go of God no matter how awful the situation.'* It is easy to say God is good when everything is going well, but what about when it feels like our lives have shattered all around us? Unwavering trust takes courageous faith – but also true honesty.

Lord, I thank You for the reminder that lament actually reflects a deep trust in You. Help me not to be afraid of it – or of speaking to my own soul when it would be useful to do so. Amen.

*Mags Duggan, *God among the Ruins* (Abingdon, UK: BRF, 2018)

His timing

READ: JOHN 11:17–27

'I am the resurrection and the life. The one who believes in me will live, even though they die' (v25)

We return today to the story of Lazarus. We have already noted that Jesus stayed away when He heard that Lazarus had become ill, because He knew God wanted to work a miracle. But what about Mary and Martha, Lazarus' sisters? They were not privy to such information. Jesus was a good friend – they had reached out to let Him know about their brother, so must have expected Him to return. They must have been so confused and disappointed when He didn't appear. And then they suffered the loss of their beloved brother... Lazarus had been dead for four days by the time that Jesus arrived. While Martha went out to see Him, Mary did not. I think I would have been inconsolable by this point – and probably very angry.

I find it so interesting that Jesus asks Martha to exercise her faith to express who she believes He is *before* her brother is raised. Often, it is in that waiting time – when we can also be dealing with a lot of pain – that displaying our faith is the most difficult and yet He is still the Messiah; He *is* the resurrection and the life.

There are many instances in our lives when we don't understand God's timing, when He seems to wait to answer our prayers – or perhaps doesn't even seem to answer them at all. I was really moved and challenged by a eulogy I heard recently. Speaker and writer Priscilla Shirer shared on social media a video of her brother speaking at their mother's funeral. He had been wrestling with God as to why He let her die and described what God said back to him: 'There were always only two answers to your prayers. Either she was going to be healed, or she was going to be healed. Either she was going to live, or she was going to live. Either she was going to be with family, or she was going to be with family. Either she was going to be well taken care of, or she was going to be well taken care of.' I certainly found that challenged my perspective.

Lord, there are times when I really don't understand what is happening, and feel the pain acutely. Help me to continue to trust You. Amen.

In the garden of despair

READ: MATTHEW 26:36–46

'My soul is overwhelmed with sorrow to the point of death.' (v38)

It is in the Garden of Gethsemane, knowing the betrayal that is about to occur and the suffering that would soon follow, that we get a glimpse of Jesus in a state of despair. The intensity of the sorrow is palpable – in Luke's account of this, he describes Jesus' sweat as being like drops of blood – a sign of truly awful anguish (Luke 22:44). There is a sense of Jesus openly wrestling not only with His emotions but also with His Father. He even asks whether the cup of suffering can be taken away from Him. In our own intense sorrow, do we pour out our feelings as honestly and openly before God?

In my own life, coming face to face with end of life suffering caused all sorts of responses in me. I had had days sitting next to my mum, working as she slept. All I longed for was for her to slip away peacefully, but that did not happen and her body began to shut down bit by bit. Watching that was agonising – and confusing, as it brought up emotions I wasn't sure how to process. It was hard to try and articulate how I was feeling, but I took comfort from reading this passage and knowing that Jesus knows what it is to feel utter despair. One of the hardest things was to be reminded that not only did He express His emotions to God, He also submitted to His will and said: 'Yet not as I will, but as you will' (v39). While everything in us may want to beg God for a swift conclusion rather than a prolonged one, it's important that we pray for His will instead, surrendering our own.

At times of despair, we can tend to cocoon ourselves, turning inwardly and even isolating ourselves. Here, we see Jesus recognised that He needed to wrestle alone before God, but also needed the support of close friends, so asked them to stay nearby. While we may get to a point of having no words to say, we can still lean on our friends and invite them into the space of our suffering.

Lord, I thank You for Your honesty in the Garden of Gethsemane. Help me to reflect on this account, and take note of the emotions it stirs as well as what You want to teach me through it. Amen.

The sting of betrayal

READ: MATTHEW 26:47–56

'Do what you came for, friend' (v50)

The scene shifts as others arrived in the garden, including Jesus' close friend Judas. He knew that He was going to be betrayed, handed over by someone who had lived and even worked right next to Him. The disappointment in His friend, and pain over the loss of that friendship, must have cut so deep – and yet Jesus responded graciously (still calling Judas 'friend'!), knowing that it was all part of His journey to the cross. Jesus taught that we should take up our 'cross daily' (Luke 9:23) but is that the way we respond when we are pierced by the thoughtless words or actions of a friend? I know that I can have a tendency to play the moment over and over in my mind, and justify the way I responded at the time and afterwards. I can also wallow in the disappointment for hours – days even. Jesus, however, was more than simply resigned; His face was set like flint (see Isa. 50:7) as He was resolute to embrace the pain of loss and then physical suffering, because He knew the final outcome.

Sometimes, we can be overwhelmed by disappointment and loss but, looking back, we can see God working through it. I can remember feeling swamped by sadness and loneliness when a friendship group I had taken so much comfort in, even though it hadn't been that supportive in reality, suddenly crumbled away. I was praying with a friend and she said she felt God had allowed it for my protection. It took a while, but I did accept that that was His wisdom and I learned to let it go.

Of course, there can be moments when we feel utter disappointment at ourselves for betraying Jesus, with our thoughts or actions (perhaps including betraying a friend). As I have shared previously, I know the sting of realising the depths of my own sinful capability as I betrayed others when I tried to find comfort for myself. If that is where you are at today, know that you are not alone. Take courage from the gracious response of Jesus, confess and open your heart to His forgiveness.

Lord, I offer up to You the pain and disappointment I have felt from the loss of friendships. Where I have felt betrayed, or have been the one betraying, help me to work through and release the negative emotions, opening myself up to Your gracious love. Amen.

21

Feeling abandoned

READ: MATTHEW 27:45–50

'My God, my God, why have you forsaken me?' (v46)

As I write today, my mum is so sedated that she probably won't come around again. The stark reality of never hearing her voice again, never sharing a moment of closeness, is beginning to sink in. The pain of loss can be so unbearable – currently, it feels more like an endurance test, as Mum has been in her final moments for over ten days and we have been sharing some of her care. We feel like we are dragging our bodies around as tiredness envelops, and everything I'm reading about grief reveals there is no let up on the lack of sleep. At such moments, we can feel totally alone, even when surrounded by other people who love us dearly.

The cross was the one place where the Saviour of the world truly *was* abandoned. His response was to cry: 'My God, my God, why have you forsaken me?' (v46). I imagine it was a deep, guttural cry of anguish, as was the other cry He did before breathing His last (v50).

This scream of inconsolable misery can be

our instinctive response to agonising loss. I have been reading Simon Thomas' book, *Love, Interrupted** – his account about the sudden loss of his wife after just a three-day battle with cancer. With a young son, he knew he couldn't fall apart, but describes how he had moments in which he had to escape to find a space in which to howl loudly. I was so moved when he expressed how close he got to throwing himself into the river as the intense grief overtook; just at that moment, he 'felt the presence of Jesus. I could feel him, just sitting beside me, crying with me'.

The Bible tells us that Jesus is able to sympathise with us as He has experienced what we do as humans (Heb. 4:15). What He uttered on the cross tells me that He understands the utter hopelessness that can grip us in our loss. I find it incredible that, in John's retelling of Jesus' crucifixion, he includes the detail of Jesus taking the time to ask John and Mary to look after one another (Luke 19:26). I believe Jesus sits with us in our pain, but also provides us with deep care.

Lord, I know You understand the pain of my deepest loss; help me to open myself to Your comfort and care. Amen.

*Simon Thomas, *Love, Interrupted* (Newark, UK: Trigger Publishing, 2019)

22

Walking the road with us

READ: LUKE 24:13–34

'Jesus himself came up and walked along with them' (v15)

Imagine the scene. Two friends, who had put their hope in Jesus and followed Him, had just witnessed His terrible crucifixion. Overcome with grief and confusion, they were now travelling back home along the road to Emmaus, unable to talk about anything other than what had just happened. They were completely enveloped by it and probably immensely disappointed that the person they thought was their Saviour was now dead. Suddenly, a stranger appeared and asked them what they were talking about. They couldn't believe He didn't know, but went on to explain.

It is so interesting to see that they were kept from recognising Jesus, but also that He chose to walk alongside them. Rather than simply revealing who He was, instead He asked them a question that gave them the opportunity to share their thoughts and feelings with Him (just as He had done with Hagar – see Day 12). He was interested in journeying *with* them, rather than simply sweeping all the pain away instantly.

As He did so, they learned more about Him and about the Scriptures (vv25–27). He provided deep revelation by explaining the Bible's overarching story of salvation and His part in it.

They were obviously drawn to Jesus because, when He went to depart from them, they urged Him to stay (vv28–29). It was as He broke bread that they recognised Him and, after He left, they eagerly told the disciples what had happened.

I don't understand why God sometimes answers our prayers for healing, or other form of release from circumstances, with a 'Not yet', but I do know we often learn more about Him and ourselves through the journey of suffering. As Romans 5:3–4 says: 'suffering produces perseverance; perseverance, character; and character, hope.'

While I believe there are some things we won't understand this side of heaven, I do wonder if we need to change the focus of our prayers. Rather than simply asking for difficult circumstances to be changed, perhaps we need to also be asking God what He wants to teach us through the disappointment and loss.

Lord, it is so comforting to know that, even when You don't reveal all of Your plans to me straightaway, that You are there journeying alongside me. Amen.

23

Preparing the way

READ: JOHN 14:1–4,15–18

'My Father's house has many rooms; if that were not so, would I have told you that I am going there to prepare a place for you?' (v2)

Jesus gathered His disciples together for a meal the night He was betrayed. Having poured out His love upon them through washing their feet, He offered them comfort. He knew that what was about to happen would confuse, upset and bewilder them. Looking at the Amplified version of these verses shows just how much richness there is in His words. In verse 1, where the NIV version says simply 'believe', the Amplified also includes the word 'trust', after which it says: 'have faith, hold on to it, rely on it, keep going.' Sometimes, we have to remind ourselves that, however much we are struggling, we do believe in our heavenly Father and the outworking of our faith is, at that time, simply putting one foot in front of the other. We are also reminded that we don't do this alone – the Father has sent us the Holy Spirit, who is described in the Amplified version as 'Helper (Comforter, Advocate, Intercessor—Counsellor, Strengthener, Standby)' (v16). Perhaps you are feeling overwhelmed today; perhaps, even though Jesus said we would not be left as orphans, that is exactly how you feel: alone and, as the Amplified includes: 'comfortless, bereaved, and helpless' (v18). If so, try and take some time to stop and meditate on the fact that the Holy Spirit has been sent specifically to you as your helper and comforter, to strengthen you and intercede on your behalf.

The first four verses make up one of the passages that I read over my mum during her last evening with us. She could not respond, but, as I continued to speak scripture over her, I knew that she was being guided by Jesus to her new home. I prayed and thanked God that He was doing that for her, but I was also comforted by reminding myself that He was taking her to a place that He had already lovingly and painstakingly prepared for her, a place she could enjoy without pain for the first time in decades.

Lord, I thank You that You took the time to let Your disciples know that You prepare a place for each one of us, but also that the Holy Spirit will comfort us. Help me to lean into His comfort today. Amen.

24

Jesus in the storm

READ: MARK 4:35–41

'the waves broke over the boat, so that it was nearly swamped. Jesus was in the stern, sleeping on a cushion.' (vv37–38)

After what seems like a long day of Jesus teaching the crowds, He and the disciples decided to cross the lake to get away. Suddenly, a storm broke out. Even though they were being buffeted relentlessly, it appears Jesus was very comfortable on His cushion – fast asleep, while all around Him were panicking.

When we have experienced an ongoing time of deep sadness, or relentless difficulties, we can be exhausted and wrung out. Every slight wave can seem enormous and so we need to be gentle on ourselves. But sometimes the waves can continue to rage on and on and we can feel we are being engulfed.

I have a friend who has experienced some deep emotional pain over recent years. Each time she is prayed for, the same picture comes: of her in a little boat in the midst of terribly choppy waters. Her boat is being swirled around all over the place – and yet there is a sense of calm and peace inside the boat. At times her response has been a sigh of resignation that the storm is going to continue raging, but she also takes some comfort from the fact that God is reminding her He is her peace – just like there is peace in the eye of a storm.

In verse 39, Jesus was able to simply say: 'Quiet! Be still!' – and immediately 'it was completely calm'. We can have a tendency to ask for His supernatural calming of the choppy waters around us, when what He actually wants us to learn is how to allow Him to still the tempestuous emotion inside of us during those stormy times. We can trust that, even though some really deep waters may rush into our lives and disquieten us, He can save us from drowning when we turn to Him. Ultimately, we recognise that God is in control, and He offers His peace to us when we feel we are being buffeted and swirled around by life itself.

Lord, there are times of such deep waters of pain that all I want to do is jump out of my boat, or cry out to You to calm the waters down. Help me to trust that You have me, and teach me that I can be calm, even in the midst of the storm. Amen.

25

Being matured

READ: JAMES 1:2-4

'the testing of your faith produces perseverance' (v3)

We have already begun to look at the concept of God using our difficulties to teach us about life's mysteries, and deepen our knowledge of Him. While we may not fully understand why, the story of Job also shows us that God allows us to be tested. I don't know whether any of us would describe the circumstances that result in devastating loss and/or disappointment as 'pure joy' (v2). However, there is a principle at work in the description James gives, which we see in the resolute faith of those being persecuted for their faith.

I recently read about a Nigerian pastor who was executed by Boko Haram. In a hostage video released before they executed him, he encouraged us all to stand firm in our faith: 'Don't cry, don't worry, but thank God for everything.' This reminds me of the encouragement we find in Hebrews 10:23: 'Let us hold unswervingly to the hope we profess, for he who promised is faithful.' Even facing death, that pastor certainly held unswervingly to his hope in God.

While we may not be called to suffer persecution to the point of death, we do all experience situations that threaten to rock our faith, such as bereavement, ill health, relationship breakdowns, money worries or prayers unanswered in the way we hope. In this passage, James reminds us that whatever 'trials' we face in this life, we can be thankful for what they are doing to our inner selves. The wrestling and the questions can actually strengthen and mature our faith, making it far more robust. The perseverance that results is what our faith needs to be complete.

Take some time today to look back over the last week. Are there situations and people that have caused you disappointment and pain? Take them before God and ask Him to help you see those trials in the light of the strengthening work He is doing in your faith. Can you begin to view them differently, perhaps even thanking Him for what you have learned through them?

Lord, I am not sure that I always approach the trials of life with pure joy, but I thank You that I can trust You are shaping my faith, deepening my character and making me more mature in You. Amen.

26

An inexplicable peace

READ: PHILIPPIANS 4:4–7

'Do not be anxious about anything, but in every situation, by prayer and petition, with thanksgiving, present your requests to God.' (v6)

We have already seen that the psalmists believed that thanksgiving was an important part of the lament journey. After expressing our sadness, writing out what we can be thankful for, as the psalmists did, can really help us when we are feeling deep emotion. I found this to be true when I was suffering from post-natal depression: a friend gently challenged a whole group of us to try and find five things to be thankful for each day and it helped me to lift my eyes to Jesus, even as I struggled. As Isaiah 61:3 says, He can make 'a crown of beauty instead of ashes, the oil of joy instead of mourning, and a garment of praise instead of a spirit of despair.' What I love about this verse is that there is a promise to those who are poor and brokenhearted: 'They will be called oaks of righteousness, a planting of the LORD for the display of his splendour.'

As we learn to rejoice in whatever circumstances we find ourselves in (Phil. 4:4), finding contentment as Paul did, we can reveal God's splendour to those around us. Although it can be inexplicable to our human minds, an attitude of thankfulness seems to be the key to our finding peace in Him.

As I mentioned on Day 9, I was really challenged by a conference speaker who talked about giving up the right to understand everything that happens. She went on to say that it is as we relinquish those rights that the 'peace of God, which transcends all understanding' (v7) is able to get to work. So often we plead with God, saying: 'If only I could understand, then I would be at peace,' but this scripture shows us that our human comprehension is not what provides peace. The Bible promises us: 'You will keep in perfect peace those whose minds are steadfast, because they trust in you' (Isa. 26:3). Jesus, calmly asleep in the storm, is our example (Matt. 8:23–27); we can be at peace and rest – even as the storms of life rage around us.

Lord, help me to truly trust You, so much so that I can rejoice whatever my circumstances and lean into Your peace rather than my own understanding. Amen.

27

From comforted to comforter

READ: 2 CORINTHIANS 1:3–5

'the God of all comfort... who comforts us in all our troubles, so that we can comfort those in any trouble with the comfort we ourselves receive from God' (vv3–4)

In His Sermon on the Mount, Jesus said: 'Blessed are those who mourn, for they will be comforted' (Matt. 5:4). It seems an odd thing to say, but also a reassuring one as we can trust that, however long our mourning lasts, however dark our days feel, He *will* comfort us. This is a promise directly from our Saviour's mouth that we can cling to in those moments when all we can do is hang on.

Sometimes, in the midst of the confusion, we can wonder exactly how that can be, and yet, strange as it can seem, our loss and disappointment can open our hearts wider, as our desperation expands our capacity to receive from Him. As God brings us His comfort we may find, over time, that we are able to reach out and share that comfort with others. I was editing a worldwide magazine and read about a woman from Guyana who lost her six-month-old daughter – she said that, while the loss was devastating and engulfing for herself, it did also open her up to the suffering of others – perhaps God can do that through our losses, in His timing of course, in a way we hadn't noticed before.

My husband and I experienced this in a different way; we had gone through a period of separation and had to face the severe disappointment that our marriage had not been as we had expected and longed for it to be. After we got back together and started counselling, we quickly found other couples approaching us who wanted to share the difficulties they were experiencing. Even though we hadn't yet finished dealing with own pain, God brought others to us. We had been brought low and humbled, and so didn't feel like we could hand out 'pat answers', but what they needed, we could provide – a safe place to be open and honest without judgment. We were so grateful for how God used our own disappointment to reach out and help others.

Lord, I do believe that You offer comfort in difficult times, and often enable us to extend that comfort outwards too. Help me to be aware of anyone You want me to reach out to today. Amen.

28

An eternal perspective

READ: 2 CORINTHIANS 4:7–18

'we fix our eyes not on what is seen, but on what is unseen' (v18)

This passage contains one of my favourite descriptions: 'we have this treasure in jars of clay' (v7). We are fragile, but there is a purpose behind that: 'to show that this all-surpassing power is from God and not from us.' We can get so frustrated and disappointed when life seems to spiral out of our own control, but when that happens we are reminded that it isn't ours to control in the first place. As Paul says, 'this happened that we might not rely on ourselves but on God' (2 Cor. 1:9).

It is what Paul says about being hard pressed but not crushed (see vv8–9) that always strikes me as incredible. If anyone had a reason to be disappointed by what he had faced, I would say Paul did. Some of his hardships included being imprisoned, flogged, beaten, stoned and shipwrecked, going hungry and living with the concern of caring for many churches (2 Cor. 11:23–28).

As I mentioned on Day 15, this passage also contains the verse that was a real comfort for my mum: 'Therefore we do not lose heart. Though outwardly we are wasting away, yet inwardly we are being renewed day by day. For our light and momentary troubles are achieving for us an eternal glory that far outweighs them all' (vv16–17). Just like the image of God collecting our tears, I visualise that the difficulties we face, including deep disappointments and losses, are fashioning us for eternity. To go back to the picture of us being jars of clay, let's remember that God is the potter and we are the work of His hand (Isa. 64:8). When we go through experiences that feel like pressure and heat, we can focus on the fact that He is shaping us for eternity. It may be that your loss is a frailty of health. Try to take some time to meditate on the above verses and remember that the pain and problems of today are 'achieving for us an eternal glory' (v17).

Lord, there are times when I feel overwhelmed by my circumstances. Help me to remember that I am the clay and You are the potter. While I may feel like much is being stripped from my life, You are actually renewing my spirit. Amen.

29

Help for our weakness

READ: ROMANS 8:18–27

'In the same way, the Spirit helps us in our weakness. We do not know what we ought to pray for, but the Spirit himself intercedes for us through wordless groans.' (v26)

As we come to the end of these devotional readings, let's remember with thanks that the suffering we face on this earth – whether loss, disappointment or any other type – will one day pale into insignificance, even though it can feel all-consuming at the time. It isn't just us but the whole of creation that is groaning, desperate for the day when we will be transformed completely into His likeness. While on earth, we live with the tension of the 'now and not yet' of the kingdom. Just like the rest of creation, our bodies know that – we groan inwardly too. We hope for what is to come, and at times wrestle with the disappointment of not seeing it as quickly as we would like. But what an incredible hope we have; to enjoy our adoption as God's children to the full by being with Him forever. That is what we have to look forward to. We can be impatient for that, which is what my mum wrestled with in her final years; every breath was a struggle and movement became so limited and painful she was desperately eager to enjoy the redemption of her body as well as come face to face with her Saviour. And yet it is in the looking forward to, in the hoping, that we learn patience, as we have seen.

God does not leave us to navigate this time of waiting though, as His 'Spirit helps us in our weakness'. While we may have moments when we are simply swamped by heartache, pain or depression, He does not stay far off. He also intercedes on our behalf with 'wordless groans'. There are times when I read that verse and think: 'I want to groan too', and I know that that is OK. In those moments when all I can do is curl up into a ball, sob and groan, He hears, He comes alongside and He comforts.

Lord, thank You for the reminder that we all, alongside creation, yearn to be reconciled to You for all eternity. Thank You that Your Spirit is with me always, and prays on my behalf. Amen.

30

An anchor for the soul

READ: HEBREWS 6:13–20

'We have this hope as an anchor for the soul, firm and secure.' (v19)

I would like to close by focusing our attention on our incredible heavenly Father and Saviour. Yes, it is important to acknowledge that we do all have struggles; yes, we endure deep suffering and immense pain at times, but we also receive His incredible mercy through the sacrifice of Jesus Christ (1 Pet. 1:3). That mercy enables us to be merciful towards others in their suffering too, as we come to understand that we are all part of His body and are here to support each other; when one of us is weak we need the tender care of those around us (Rom. 5:1–7).

It is so interesting to read about Jesus that: 'Son though he was, he learned obedience through what he suffered and, once made perfect, he became the source of eternal salvation for all who obey him' (Heb. 5:8–9). We are in good company when we suffer, and can remind ourselves of its greater purpose. If Jesus learned from His suffering, my prayer is that we will be quick learners too.

Let's also remember that we don't walk through any part of our lives alone, but have the 'God of all comfort' (2 Cor. 1:3) guiding us. And He has provided a living hope that we can rejoice in and also cling hold of as 'an anchor for the soul'. As the passage in Hebrews 6 reminds us, He is trustworthy and unchanging and so we can know deep down in our souls that we can trust Him, even when the storms of life cause us to wonder if He is there anymore.

Finally, I want to echo what Paul says in Romans 15:13: 'May the God of hope fill you with all joy and peace as you trust in him, so that you may overflow with hope by the power of the Holy Spirit.' Your heart may not feel like it is bursting with joy at times, but be assured that God's peace and His hope transcend our circumstances, and lift your eyes heavenward, where one day disappointment and loss will be gone forever.

Lord, I thank You for the reminder that You too learned through Your suffering, and it is through Your resurrection that I have the hope that anchors my soul. Teach me to grab hold of that anchor all the days of my life. Amen.

Discover the full Insight range

Discover our full range of Insight resources and courses, all of which provide accessible and practical insights on tough issues that so many of us face in our lives today. The series has been developed to help people understand and work through these key issues, drawing on real-life case studies, biblical examples and counselling practices. Whether for yourself or to help support someone you know, we have one-off Insight books, courses and daily devotionals on key topics. Find out more at **cwr.org.uk/insight**

These Three Things:
Finding your Security, Self-worth and Significance

How do you sum up, in one book, content that covers our deep spiritual needs, personal motivations, and revival? Homesickness and belonging? Our disconnection, isolation and reconnection with God and others in our increasingly 'contactless' society? Let's start by going back to the original plan: who God is, and who we are; where it all went wrong, and how we find our way back; what it is we're looking for, and how and where to find it; all while daring to ask the questions:

- Who am I?
- Do I matter?
- What's the point?

Find out more and order at **cwr.org.uk/ttt**

Free online resources available for groups and churches

There's something for everyone!

Find God in your everyday

If you love to spend time with God, then why not take ten extra minutes to hear from God and understand His Word? CWR's range of Bible reading notes include something for everyone, including *Every Day with Jesus*, *Inspiring Women Every Day*, and Jeff Lucas' *Life Every Day*.

Find out more at **cwr.org.uk/store**

Courses and seminars

Waverley Abbey College

Publishing and media

Conference facilities

Transforming lives

CWR's vision is to enable people to experience personal transformation through applying God's Word to their lives and relationships.

Our Bible-based training and resources help people around the world to:

- Grow in their walk with God
- Understand and apply Scripture to their lives
- Resource themselves and their church
- Develop pastoral care and counselling skills
- Train for leadership
- Strengthen relationships, marriage and family and much more.

CWR Applying God's Word to everyday life and relationships

CWR, Waverley Abbey House,
Waverley Lane, Farnham,
Surrey GU9 8EP, UK

Telephone: +44 (0)1252 784700
Email: info@cwr.org.uk
Website: cwr.org.uk

Registered Charity No. 294387
Company Registration No. 1990308

Our insightful writers provide daily Bible reading notes and other resources for all ages, and our experienced course designers and presenters have gained an international reputation for excellence and effectiveness.

CWR's Training and Conference Centre in Surrey, England, provides excellent facilities in idyllic settings – ideal for both learning and spiritual refreshment.